Cannabis: Bonsai Growing Techniques and Why

By: Lavoy Allison

Copyright © Lavoy Allison

Thank you for your purchase of this book. I do hope that you purchase it and do not find some ill way of getting it. Not only is that how capitalism works but Lord God intended for us to work for what we get. Thank you and have a Blessed Day.

Dedication

To: Selena the love of my life. Thank you for loving me more than any woman has and putting up with my wise cracks. I do it to see you laugh and that beautiful smile. Cheese wiz is pretty awesome though.

To: My family for saying nothing while I studied the cannabis plant and laughing with me when things went right. I love all of you birth family and foster families too.

To: My readers for everything that you do to inspire your own happiness and over come the illness that brought you to buy this book!

Table of Contents

Chapter 1: Cannabis the Multi-Use Medicine

I would like to say that everyone knows that cannabis is the most used medicine that we can think of. Sadly that is not the fact. It may be another ten years before people realize that the process of separating THC to make pills made up 60% of the medicine that people take. Why have they been able to keep that from us? It was patented and that keeps the government or anyone else from talking about it. Besides other than the side affects from the solution used to separate the THC to keep you from feeling "high," most medicine worked fine.

I want to tell you more about 'modern' medicine that they haven't told you. Many of the ingredients used to make our medicine has been imported and you won't believe why we have the side affects we do! There is a place in Louisiana on the Missouri river called Cancer Alley. In Cancer Alley they still produce things close to DDT the chemicals outlawed in the United States for use on anything. Especially our food crops. Where do they sell it you ask? In Mexico, India, Asia and other third world countries that it is legal to grow

Opium, Cannabis, Effedrin and anything else they use to make our medicine.

So why the push for people to be able to use cannabis here in the United States? What hasn't been answered already? Knowing that a chemical similar to DDT is being used on our medicine and the fact, to be truthful, you can judge the dosage and use less cannabis smoking for some illnesses. Say you have a bad back ache and you don't have time to let other medicines kick in or the eatable form either. You can just take a few hits and go about your house cleaning provided you haven't over used the medicine already.

So what took the government so long to correct the problem? You have heard about lobbiest paying elected officials to vote their way. Well Surgeon Generals can be lobbied as well. I have had a lot to do with getting laws passed to keep elected officials from taking these payments and doctors from prescibing based on what pill company gave them the most money for each presciption.

I was also recruited by the CIA to work at legallizing some of the street drugs that come from medicines to cut government insurance costs. I am proud to say that I have been an avocate to legal cannabis and cut down on the number of deaths the pill companies are causing based on side affects they knew about when the drug hit the market. Other medicines used as street drugs can be very dangerous if used too much so I am slow about talking about them because of their effects of overdose can kill people like Opium and Meth which the main ingredient is effedrin.

The ingredient in Meth, effedrin, can cure the flu in a day and pneumonia as well but doctors voted to take it off the streets in the form of Heads Up pills also known as 'speed' or 'White Crosses.' I saved a heifer cow from death with just 6 pills from a Heads Up bottle which was 75% efedrin back in 1995. She had pneumonia and was staggering and couldn't walk. She has two calves the last time I saw her years ago. I have asked that they used high dosages of effedrin to treat and get rid of the Cornavirus but none is listening yet. I am still working on it.

Back to the cannabis and the 'Dugout,' to understand a few hits being enough to take the pain away. You have to look at the fact that I use for the medical purpose and haven't really smoked to get high. I tried it a few times but being the only one buying the weed is no fun. I use what they call a one hitter which you can buy with a Dugout. The one hitter looks like a straight pipe painted like a cigarette many times. A Dugout is a wooden box that holds the one hitter on one side and your cannabis on the other. Why do I use a Dugout you ask with all the ways to smoke cannabis? It is simple. I use less cannabis and save money! You waste less cannabis as well.

 So what are we looking at with President Donald Trump signing in for farmers to grow hemp? We are looking at the chance for the United States to be a major power in the medical prescription industry and having medicine sold all over the world with the American Food and Drug Administration standards which means the world will be a safer place. I have to say God bless him. He is the first president I have dealt with that is trying to help the United States take a stand in the medicine industry.

 I have been working and serving the United States in letters to the government and other duties since President George Bush Senior. I was in grade school when I started writing the government and went active duty working with the CIA in 1995. It has been a hard road seeing that I got poisoned and had to learn to read, write, and talk again while in the service. Since the release of the first edition of this book they have come up with a 'drug' that keeps people from passing HIV. I have found that cannabis cures a many ills including voices and some pain in treating myself. Also in treating myself I found that broken bones heal quicker if you eat enough. I ate a quarter ounce and I had full movement of my broken shoulder in two weeks.

 I was poisoned and had to learn to read, write, and talk again. Think about that. That was some down time but six months later I pulled myself together and wrote the Surgeon General in 1996 and two weeks later they announced that with the help of Honorary Doctor Willie Lavoy Allison they were legalizing cannabis in California for medical purposes. Medically speaking anyone that feels the 'need' to get high and not just wants to get high has a medical (usually mental) issue and need medical cannabis. Poisons in drugs even being around gas fumes too long will lead to needing to meicate or get high. As far as gas fumes the old blue label rice made Zima worked great too.

Those that are getting 'high' on K2 (which is tobacco insecticide that contains embalming fluid). They are getting mental illnesses and cancer and will need cannabis too. I don't get the 'high' killing yourself but you can see many know that it is killing them but they keep doing it. They need the cannabis excape. They have suicidal intentions and need cannabis. The reason states are going to recreational cannabis is so people do not have to worry about their medical records coming up or their illness when asked if they use cannabis to get a job. Also so the government doesn't have to worry so much about medical bills when people are using cannabis to do their thing on their own dime.

Chapter 2: Things You Need to Know About Growing Cannabis

There is a lot about cannabis that even seasoned growers are still learning. I have looked at many pictures and even dispenaries are not getting the highest yield they could get. But not to worry I will release to you my growing secrets in this book! It doesn't matter if you are growing commerical hemp or medical cannabis you need to read this book.

I have taught people how to grow their cannabis so that when you shake the bud against a table THC powder falls off to make a pill and still there is so much THC that you can't see the green in the bud. How you might ask and why? I use powdered sugar everytime I water. See in photosinathises the plant makes a sugar for it to feed on. Adding sugar adds the needed ingredients to produce THC.

Now the why? The human body's bone marrow produces a sugar to feed on much like the plants. Bone marrow produces our red and white blood cells which feeds the body and prevents and fights germs in the body. The food bone marrow produces for itself has 13 elements and THC has 16 elements. The extra three are T-H-C. They are for the natural pain killer and laxitive as well as other uses. So you can see as a honorary doctor there are uses for the medicine to fight HIV, AIDS, and Cancer if you don't wait too long. As i revise this book for the second edition of it they have a drug to keep people from passing HIV through sex that probably wasn't thought of until someone read this book. With the deaths involved and havoc the diseses have caused you would think this information doctors would tell you freely but the pharmaceutical companies have been fighting it all the way.

 I am only an honorary doctor. But I can say from personal experience that medical cannabis that is pure and not sprayed with anything will make the voices stop. When I got poisoned I was hearing voices and seeing things too. Cannabis was the only cure I had. I spent four years on probation because I used cannabis in Tennessee to get better. While I was in the service of my country I thought it was my job to stop some people poisoning others and their law enforcement families letting them and helping them get away with it.

Hopefully so far is enough for you to understand the history behind legalizing cannabis and why. Ready to grow bud? What about hemp? I want you to know that cannabis can and will be a plant that needs care. You are going to get your hands a little dirty but the time put in is well worth it. I wish I had the pictures taken of all the plants I have grown and be able to show you how much I have learned through my bonsai techniques and their affects on the growth and yield but I can't. I can show you the last plant I grew though. I found it on Google with the Getty Images logo on it from where I uploaded it to Twitter.

I left the plant and the pictures in Tennessee when I moved to Florida to get started on legalizing cannabis here. With some help it happened.

  If you will take a look at the cannabis plant above you may see the same thing I do. This plant has not been trimmed or 'topped enough. If you have rasied tobacco' to produce a high yield you know what I am talking about. What do I mean you ask? The plant doesn't have thick foliage and it looks like it is developing bud already so it is to old to trim to increase the yield. Look at the following photo.

D
o
yo
u

see a stem in this photo? No because the plants
have been trimmed and cut back to force them
to grow more foliage or leaves. Why do you
need more leaves? Because the leaves help
feed the plant while it produces the fruit which
is the bud. The plants in the picture above will
yield a high amount which is what you want.

 So how do I increase my yield? Lets look at
the picture below.

Wh
at
you
see
here
is

the top shoot of the plant. Myself I would cut

where the three leaves meet and eat what you cut off or use it to clone the plant. It tastes better than turnip greens. Don't think it will get you high at this stage because it won't. The plant doesn't start to produce THC until it is close to the budding stage which can take six-eight months depending on how long you keep it in the vegetation stage with 14-16 hours of light a day.

 Back to the trimming, each limb will have a top or end that needs to be trimmed. But you are not done there. You still need to trim the tips of each leaf to get the plant to feel it needs more leaves. Look at this picture.

You see the black lines on each leaf. That is where you should be cutting each leaf every week. The plant does grow the leaf ends back if I remember correctly and again they are good to eat. I eat them as I cut them off but you can cook them if you like. I didn't have a chance to use salad dressing but I am sure they would make a great salad. Those techniques is where I come up with the title. As you would a bonsai you trim and pinch the tips of the plant limbs and in this case the leaves to get the cannabis plant to produce more.

While I haven't added in wiring up a bonsai style cannabis plant it can be done if you want to sacrifice that plant's yield. Yes you can grow a cannabis bonsai but you must keep it pot bound. Also you have to grow it close to the lighting your use for the plant because by nature the plant grows to the light. To do it right you need a LED light that is full spectrum you can place on the desktop or growing surface close to the plant. The closer you can get your light the better. If you plan to wire it to make it grow in a different direction or shape do so while it is young. Remember that if you cut a large branch or the main stem they are hollow and will need treatment.

Chapter 3: Growing Bud Without Seeds

Growers today spend a lot of time researching how to get the most THC out of their whole yield. And it is paying off. Why? Because that is where the medicine is and the high dollar payout whether it be selling it or medicating using less cannabis. That means either growing the male and female plants separate or just grow female plants. The males produce pollen and the females produce the bud or fruit. The female is the only plant that produces THC. There is even research into how far a male plant has to be from a female plant for it not to fertilize it and cause seeds to grow.

Why would you not want seeds to grow more plants. Because you can clone or take cuttings from a female plant and only get females. That is the great part about it and trust me the cannabis plant is not hard to clone. You just go to Wal-Mart or even Amazon buy rooting hormone powder. Cut off a clipping of the plant dip it in the powder and stick it in the soil. Keep it wet and in a few months it will start growing. Just remember to keep a stick beside it to know when it starts getting taller. You might want to take pictures as well. That way you know it is growing and you will know when to start trimming the leaves.

  Remember each state has different laws about how many plants you can have so be aware of them. Besides if you follow the growing techniques above you will yield enough bud and leaves off one plant that you will have to give some away to stay on the dry bud limit. Now wouldn't that be nice? It will happen trust me.

  If I was you I would find another grower that you can get a cutting or clone from to make sure you get a female. Another way to get a female to the Seed Bank that promises to sale female seeds. I have never used them but there is probably some truth in it. Once I had grew some plants from seeds from where I bought some cannabis on the street. Needless to say that I wasn't lucky enough to have two females and I couldn't find anyone that knew the difference either. I ended up with seeds because I couldn't tell the plants apart until it was too late. Good reason to clone so you can over time have nothing but females.

Chapter 4: Cloning Female Cannabis Plants

In the last chapter I talked some about cloning. In this chapter I am going to try to explain it in better detail. As I said before you will want to learn to clone to keep from having seeds in your cannabis. Without cloning you will have to grow from seeds and that is always a chance. A chance that you might have a male in your females which will pollinate your females and produce seeds.

As I said before cloning is not that hard. You stare at your plant to find where and what you are willing to do without. If you have ever topped tobacco then you know about 'sucker' limbs that drain the plant of needed nutrients and cause it to not produce as much. A cannabis plant does the same thing and those suckers make good clones. If you have never topped tobacco then you wait until the cannabis plant is about two to three months old and at the stalk of the plant there will be two limbs coming from the same place. Cut the smaller ones out to use as your clones. If you have enough clones then leave them and keep their ends and leaves trimmed.

Now that you have your cuttings or clones you need to keep them wet until you can get them in the pot and soil you start them in. This process from; cutting it off the plant, to getting it in the soil should not take over ten minutes. And that is if you stop to take a break and go to the bathroom. As I said you should keep the cuttings wet until they get the rooting hormone if you choose to use it. I usually don't use it on cannabis I just put them in the soil and keep them wet.

So let's talk about what you are going to need to do your cloning. Note that cloning and taking cuttings is the same thing. Just remember to cut at a 45 degree angle. The best way to get the job done fast and right is to have every thing ready before you start. You need a cup or glass of water depending on how long you want your cuttings. You need a sharp blade to cut the plant with, and your pots or cups with the soil already in them.

In my first edition of this book published in 2019 I received a bad review because I trust eating cannabis and mentioned Miracle Grow as a suitable rooting hormone and potting soil. If you are worried about it being organic don't use any rooting hormone at all. It will still grow fine as along as you keep the soil wet. As far as soil I have used Miracle Grow soil and fertilizer for years on tomatoes but if you have an organic substance to use please do.

You will get differ ent view points from differ ent peopl

e. I believe it doesn't matter what kind of rooting hormone or soil you get as far as Miracle Grow goes. But others will say that Clonex is more organic. But like I said you can do without rooting hormone. Look at this Fast Root from Miracle Grow on Amazon. It sells for $5.97 and is a great deal. As you can see it is a dry powder so when you pull your cuttings or clones from the cup or glass of water you know the hormone is going to stick to the stem. Then you just take a pencil and make a hole in your soil in your pot and pack the dirt around it like this. For $5 with Clonex you get a gel pack that you can't reseal as far as I remember. I really don't like the fact that you can't reseal the package and it is for one time use.

This is what you cutting will look like in the soil. Notice the 45 degree angle cut on the bottom marked 'A'.

You will also need the pot and soil ready for your cuttings. I prefer Miracle Grow myself because it is fertilized and balanced and grows cannabis real well. I have grown a plant for someone that wanted neutral soil and used hydroponic fertilizer. Some prefer an organic fertilizer which is great too. You will want to start with a small pot until it has time to develop. Some people use the Dixie cups that you drink out of and this is fine. Just make sure you have holes in the bottom for it to drain the extra water out. It will only be there about two months if that. Everyone is going to have different results because of using different nutrients and light settings.

Now with your things all together, the pot full of soil, a pencil so that you can create the hole the cuttings in going into, some rooting hormone in a plastic sandwich bag (you don't want to contaminate your whole jar of rooting hormone when you use it), and your blade to cut your branches you are ready to take your cuttings. At this time you are ready to study your plant again and make sure where you want your cuttings taken from and how long you want them. Why? Because you can't have do overs.

Try to have your mother plant as close to your other needed items as you can or at least have a cup of water with enough water to cover the ends of your cuttings. You do not want to make a cut and then let the end of your cutting dry out because it will die. And the thing about it, the time it takes to die may be a week or two before it shows. That can give a beginner the wrong idea as to what killed the cutting. And remember you only have so many cuttings you can take from a mother plant at a time which depends on the growth stage

While we are talking about your mother plant some people like to use a certain plant to take cuttings from and they do not plan on getting smoke bud or shake-(leaves) from it. You may take this route if you like. I can't say that I have so like I said you can always take the 'sucker limbs' as your cuttings and clone the plant from there. Also when you first trim the main limbs and the main stem by cutting the ends off to make it grow more you can make those ends your cuttings.

I guess I need to show you a picture to explain what I am talking about. I don't want this to be confusing to some or all even. I have the picture labeled A, B, and C where the (A) labeled the 'sucker limbs', (B) is the main branches that get trimmed and 'C' is the trunk or stem of the plant.

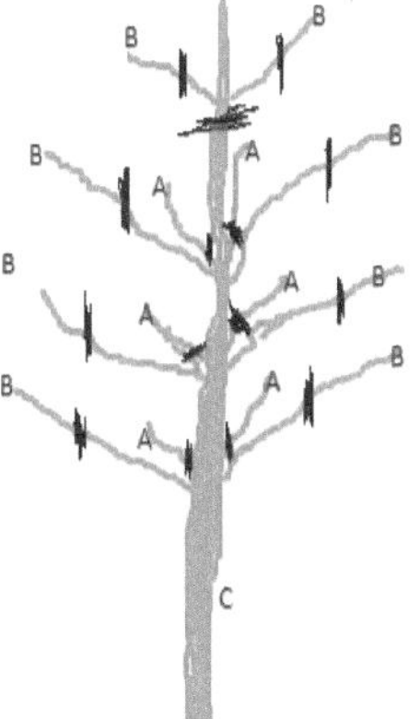

A: Is the sucker limbs I have been telling you about. THe black lines are where you cut them as close to the stalk as you can.

B: Is the main branches and the black marks on them are where you trim the plant at about 4-5 months to force it to grow more foliage and limbs.

C: Is the stem where the plant grows from the ground up on most planets!

As you can see in the diagram there are plenty of places that you can take cuttings from. Even if you don't need anymore cuttings you need to take a look at these cuts. As I said you have to trim a plant to confuse it to think it needs more branches and leaves to survive. It is like that regular trimming of a bonsai. Here you need to check your plant every week or two to see if you need to trim it.

In the picture below you will need to make a 45 degree cut (Marked B:) on your cutting to get it to take root easier. Also you need to have this cut about a half inch to an inch below the last set of nodes on your cutting as in this next picture marked (C:). Remember that the nodes are where leaves or small branches were and your roots are going to be. You cut the bottom set of leaves off so that the nodes can go into the ground to form your roots. You now have a cutting and it is a clone of the mother plant.

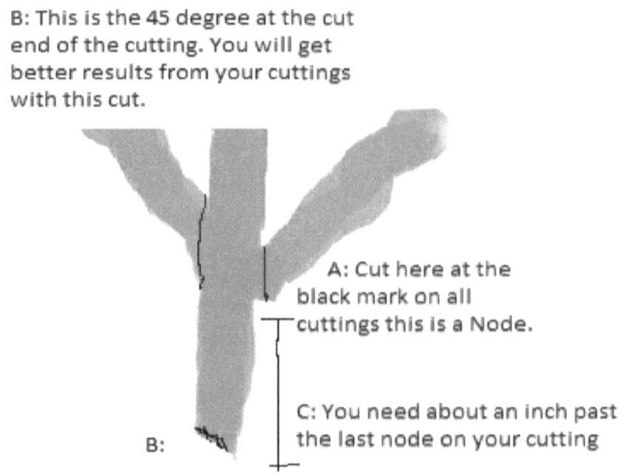

  Now make sure your soil is packed well in the pot. Take your pencil and bore a hole deep enough to get your cuttings in the soil up passed the nodes. Now you just take your cutting from the cup or glass of water and stick the cut end into the plastic bag with the rooting hormone you poured out of your main container. Close off the bag with your fingers and give it a shake so that the part of the cutting that is going into the ground is covered with rooting hormone. If you choose to not

have rooting hormone just put the wet cutting
into the soil.

  You have now successfully cloned a mother
cannabis plant. Remember to keep it sprayed
with water and the soil it is in moist. Soon you
will start the process over with that cutting
when it becomes a mother plant.

Chapter 5: Caring For Your Clone as It Grows

So now you have your clone in the pot and you have kept it watered and moist. You have been checking the height regularly and noticed that it has started to grow. Good so soon it it will be time to check your root growth and see if it is getting root bound. Becoming root bound is where the roots have grown so much that they are circling around inside the pot. Usually you keep an eye on them and when they start becoming root bound you repot the plant (the cutting has roots it is officially a plant now). If you notice that roots are going around the root ball you might want to make cuts along the root ball through the roots to keep the roots from choking the plant.

So now you are looking for a bigger pot than you started with. Since you are working to have the plant to produce more foliage and bud you need to make sure that it will be able to hold the weight up in the air. The roots gripping the soil ball is the only way it can naturally do that. Also you want the plant to make the best use of the soil in the pot.

I will give you three guesses as to what you do next! Now that the plant is growing you need to trim the new growth and trim the leaves as I showed you before. Yes you can eat them and they are good! I wouldn't try to get a cutting from a newly rooted plant so just do some trimming to get the plant in fear so it will produce more foliage or leaves. But since you probably only had a few leaves on it when you take your cutting you will not be doing as heavey of a pruning or trimming job. At this point if you want to do it right you will have the LED (low heat light) as close as possible to grow thick foilage as soon as it grows roots.

From there the process as you can see starts all over again and all you do is work your way up repotting it until you get to about 4-6 months . You will have it in the biggest pot you want to use by the time it starts to smell. Just keep trimming, just keep trimming, and you will have more cannabis than you can handle. Especially if you are not going to be eating it. I like my leaves dried out and in milk right out of the microwave. It will ease some pain and make the grump in you take on a smiling fever!

I titled this book "Bonsai Growing

Techniques and Why" because what you just read is the same way you care for a bonsai. The only difference is you allow a cannabis plant to get as big as it can over time. You are just restricting its growth at first to make it sprout more limbs and foliage. As I said it is much like topping tobacco but you do more with cannabis. You trim the leaves as well.

Chapter 6: Lighting For Your Cannabis

Most of us understand that plants need light to live. If you skipped that day of class to smoke in the restroom you should pay attention. And $30 the next time you see the offering plate come by because that education you must have not valued was your gift from the Lord. Now that you made amends I will explain how to provide for your cannabis, another gift from the Lord you should use but not abuse.

Well many of us are forced to grow indoors and there is a lot of talk about the best lights to use. I prefer the full spectrum LED lights for indooor growing. There again If I was living where the light I used had to produce heat for the plant then I would do things differently. That is when I would switch to a sodium or halogen light that produces heat and light too. The thing about it you usually can't get the full spectrum light rays in one bulb which means it costs more to operate.

What is full spectrum light rays and why is it important? You want your plant to get the same type light rays as the sun provides for plants in nature which is defined as full spectrum. It is very important for your plants through the growing stages. As I said the LED full spectrum light doesn't put off much heat. In close environments it is important not to have a lot of heat because it will evaporate the water right out of the soil and burn your plants. If you are using a closed in space or grow tent you will need to keep the air flowing because the tent will build up heat and the plant pots will dry out fast. I had to water daily even indoors.

Now that you know the reasons behind picking a light you need to decide your budget and you need an idea of where you want to have your grow area. If you have an out building to grow in and it gets cold during the winter you will want a sodium or halogen light to produce heat so you don't have to provide for heat during the winter as well. If you had to supply a heater and electric for the heater in the winter that would be extra that a heated growing light would take care of.

How long do you leave the light on? Well that depends on you, your light bill, and the growing stage the plant is in. If you chose the

LED light then you are in luck because they usually have a built in inverter so they do not use as much power. The sodium and halogen you better have a second income to pay the light bill from what I hear.

 Back to how long you leave your lights on. Again like I said that depends on you. The three foot tall plant I had I used two different settings on my timer. I am talking about the plant that I used all these techniques on to get two pounds of shake. I split it into two different lighting lengths. For the stage from clone to a cannabis plant when it starts to smell like smoke-able bud I left the light on for 14-16 hours a day. That is know as the vegetation stage where the plant focuses on producing leaves, stems and limbs.

 The next stage is known as the flowering stage. That is where you will wait until the plant starts to smell like someone smoked a joint in the room and you will turn the light back to 8-12 hours a day so that the plant can develop the bud we potheads like so much!?! Personally I can smoke the shake just as well. How? Because if you haven't used the growing techniques I have taught you in this book you don't understand shake or the leaves of cannabis being as strong and having almost as much THC as the bud!

To sum it up as soon as you have a 2-3 week old female plant from a cutting you need to start adding powdered sugar to the watering can and mixing it up when you water the plant. As soon as you notice growth it has roots and you can add the sugar. You have to keep the leaves and limbs trimmed so that the plant is in fear of dying so it produces more foliage and bud. Keep it watered and fertilized every two to three weeks with liquid fertilizer. The last and also important step is make sure you keep your light timer on at the same time every day.

Follow this training list and you will be rolling the best cannabis you have ever smoked, eaten, or sold in your life. If you are growing hemp now that President Donald Trump has made it legal to farm hemp you will want to follow the trimming and pruning steps on a regular basis. You will have a strong crop. Remember most hemp farmers are just going to sow the seeds and let them grow. But they will only get maybe two ounces per plant and not two pounds per plant!

Thank you for reading my book and learning

from me. Have a blessed life and smoke 'em if you have them!